WORKBOOK

For

Will I Ever Be Good Enough?:

Healing Daughters of Narcissistic Mothers

Irene Franklin

Table of Contents

HOW TO USE THIS WORKBOOK

Welcome to Dr. Karyl McBride Ph.D.'s companion workbook, Will I Ever Be Good Enough?: Healing the Daughters of Narcissistic Mothers. This workbook is intended to help you interact with the book's subject at a deeper level. It attempts to help you heal from the impacts of narcissistic mothering by summarizing key chapters, emphasizing important insights, presenting self-reflection questions, giving life-changing tasks, and prompting self-evaluation.

This companion worksheet is meant to support Will I Ever Be Good Enough?. It is not a replacement for the original material, but rather a tool to help you better understand and implement its concepts. Please utilize this worksheet in combination with the book to obtain a thorough knowledge and improve your recovery process.

Guidelines for using the workbook:

- Chapter Summaries: Each chapter summary summarizes the key topics and ideas from the relevant chapter in Will I Ever Be Good Enough?. Use these summaries to refresh your memory or rapidly review key points before beginning the workbook tasks.

- Primary Takeaways: After reading each chapter summary, make a note of the primary takeaways that connect with you. These insights are designed to help you reflect on the book's themes and apply its lessons in your own life.

- Self-Reflection Questions: Following each chapter summary, you will discover self-reflection questions meant to encourage introspection and help you better understand your experiences and healing process. Take your time pondering these questions and consider writing your responses for clarity.

- Life-Changing Exercises: The workbook contains a range of exercises based on the teachings from Will I Ever Be Good Enough? These activities are designed to help you put the book's teachings into practice, stimulate personal growth, and cultivate self-compassion. Choose workouts that speak to you and incorporate them into your daily routine to get long-term results.

- Self-Evaluation Questions: At the end of the workbook, you'll discover self-evaluation questions to help you track your progress and reflect on your improvement as you go through the material. Use these questions to evaluate your successes, identify areas for improvement, and establish objectives for continued personal development.

OVERVIEW

Dr. Karyl McBride's Will I Ever Be Good Enough?: Healing the Daughters of Narcissistic Mothers is a caring and intelligent handbook for women who have grown up with narcissistic mothers. The book delves into the mental harm caused by moms who prioritize their personal wants over their daughters' emotional well-being. These moms frequently engage in manipulative, domineering, and self-centered actions, leaving their daughters feeling inadequate, unloved, and always seeking approval. McBride uses years of therapeutic practice and personal insight to provide a road to recovery for people touched by this poisonous dynamic.

The book's central theme is that daughters of narcissistic moms frequently suffer profound emotional traumas. They grow up in an atmosphere where their needs are ignored or overpowered by their mother's desire for attention, admiration, or affirmation. As a result, these girls face challenges such as poor self-esteem, perfectionism, self-doubt, and even self-sabotage. They frequently absorb their mother's criticism and neglect, convinced that they are never good enough. This deeply ingrained idea can appear in a variety of ways throughout their life, influencing their employment, relationships, and general sense of self-esteem.

The book explores at the various forms that mother narcissism may manifest. Some narcissistic moms are blatantly domineering, demanding continuous attention and praise from their children, but others may be more subtle, influencing their daughters via guilt, shame, or emotional detachment. McBride explains these dynamics and identifies particular patterns of conduct that have molded their lives.

The book focuses heavily on the long-term effects of this sort of mothering on daughters. Many women raised by narcissistic moms either overachieve to get their mother's favor or engage in self-sabotage, believing that no matter what they accomplish, they will never be good enough. These tendencies frequently continue into adulthood, influencing sexual relationships, friendships, and career interests. McBride also discusses some women's dread of becoming like their moms when they become parents, as well as strategies to stop the pattern.

Despite the terrible emotional toll, the book's overall theme is one of hope and healing. McBride provides practical methods girls may take to extricate themselves from their narcissistic moms' emotional dominance. This includes recognizing narcissistic behavior patterns, establishing healthy boundaries, and working towards self-acceptance. Understanding that the daughter's worth is not dependent on her mother's acceptance or rejection is an important step in the healing process.

The book also examines the role of therapy in healing the profound scars left by mother narcissism. Daughters may begin to recover their identities and develop lives free of their mother's narcissism by engaging in self-reflection, emotional work, and the establishment of healthy boundaries. Will I ever be good enough? provides both a thorough explanation of the issue and a hopeful, practical approach to healing and emotional rehabilitation.

CHAPTER 1: EMOTIONAL BURDEN YOU CARRY

Chapter Summary:

In this chapter, Dr. McBride delves into the intense emotional suffering that daughters of narcissistic mothers frequently endure throughout their lives. These weights might show as feelings of inadequacy, poor self-esteem, and an unending desire for acceptance. Many girls grow up feeling it is their fault if their mother is unable to love them unreservedly. The emotional neglect and manipulation they experience might lead to perfectionism or self-sabotage in adulthood. This chapter teaches readers about the weight they bear and how it affects their emotional and psychological well-being.

Key takeaways:

- Daughters frequently bear a secret emotional load of guilt and inadequacy.

- Many people assume their mother's lack of affection is their fault.

- Emotional neglect has a long-term influence on self-esteem.

- The load promotes perfectionism or self-sabotage.

- Recognizing that you have an emotional load is the first step toward healing.

- Emotional distress is frequently profoundly absorbed.

- This load has an impact on relationships, self-esteem, and mental health.

- Recognizing the weight is the first step towards healing.

Self-Reflective Questions:

What emotional baggage do you carry from your connection with your mother?

_____

_____

_____

_____

_____

_____

How has your mother's actions affected your self-esteem?

_____

_____

_____

_____

_____

_____

In what ways do you seek acceptance from others, reflecting your connection with your mother?

_____

_____

_____

_____

_____

_____

How do you deal with emotions of inadequacy?

_____

_____

_____

_____

_____

_____

_____

_____

What emotions do you struggle to express, and why?

_____

_____

_____

_____

_____

How would your life alter if you let go of your emotional

burden?

_____

_____

_____

_____

_____

_____

_____

_____

Life-changing Exercises:

Keep a journal on how your mother's influence affects you emotionally.

Write a letter to your younger self, providing affirmation and affection.

Practice daily affirmations that promote your value, regardless of whether your mother agrees.

Identify one perfectionistic propensity and take a little move toward overcoming it.

Make a note of the emotional loads you've absorbed and question their veracity.

Meditate on self-compassion and enable yourself to feel worthwhile.

Share your tale with a trustworthy friend or therapist.

Begin practicing forgiveness for yourself, rather than for your mother.

Set a boundary to safeguard your emotional well-being.

Make a list of your strengths and read them every day.

CHAPTER 2: THE EMPTY MIRROR: MY MOTHER AND I

Chapter Summary:

This chapter looks into the notion of the "empty mirror," which represents the absence of emotional reflection and approval from a narcissistic mother. Daughters with narcissistic moms may feel invisible since their emotional needs are disregarded. The mother's self-centeredness leaves little place for the daughter's personality or emotions. The daughter's self-worth becomes dependent on external affirmation, leaving her with a profound sense of emptiness and inadequacy.

Key takeaways:

- Narcissistic moms frequently fail to address their daughters' emotional needs.
- The "empty mirror" represents the daughter's lack of affirmation.

- Daughters frequently feel invisible in the relationship.

- This invisibility creates emotions of inadequacy and low self-esteem.

- External approval becomes a replacement for parental affection.

- The daughter's emotional needs are hardly satisfied.

- The absence of reflection creates a gap in the daughter's identity.

- Healing entails discovering internal affirmation and self-worth.

Self-Reflective Questions:

How did your mother's lack of emotional reflection effect your self-esteem?

_____

_____

_____

_____

_____

How do you seek external affirmation to fill the "empty mirror"?

_____

_____

_____

_____

_____

_____

How do you feel when your emotional needs are neglected?

_____

_____

_____

_____

_____

_____

What strategies have you attempted to get your mother's attention or approval?

_____

_____

_____

_____

_____

_____

_____

How has your connection with your mother affected your sense of self?

_____

_____

_____

_____

_____

_____

What would it be like to validate your own feelings and needs?

_____

_____

_____

_____

_____

_____

Life-changing Exercises:

Reflect on times when you felt invisible in your connection with your mother.

Write a letter to yourself that acknowledges your feelings and needs.

Practice internal validation by reinforcing your value on a regular basis.

Identify one area where you rely on external approval and redirect it to self-acceptance.

Create a mirror ritual in which you stare into your own eyes and express warmth and empathy.

Journal about occasions when your emotional needs were ignored.

Write a caring answer to the aspects of yourself that feel invisible.

Practice being emotionally present with oneself, providing comfort as required.

Set the desire to cease seeking acceptance from those who do not satisfy your needs.

Focus on developing self-worth from inside, regardless of your mother's influence.

CHAPTER 3: THE FACES OF MATERNAL NARCISSISM

Chapter Summary:

This chapter describes how narcissistic moms exhibit themselves, ranging from overt to covert narcissism. Overt narcissistic moms are dominating and bossy, requiring continuous attention and praise. Covert narcissistic moms, on the other hand, may look selfless while gradually manipulating their daughters via guilt, emotional isolation, or subtle violence. Understanding the many types of narcissism helps daughters identify the precise dynamics at work in their own relationships.

Key takeaways:

- Maternal narcissism can emerge in a variety of ways, both overt and covert.
- Overt narcissistic moms are dominating and attention-seeking.

- Covert narcissistic moms influence softly, frequently using guilt.

- Covert narcissism's contradictory messages frequently confuse daughters.

- Recognizing the type of narcissism helps us comprehend the mother's actions.

- Narcissists, whether overt and covert, put their own demands over those of their daughters.

- Emotional isolation and passive-aggression are common features of covert narcissistic behavior.

- Understanding these interactions is critical to recovery.

Self-Reflective Questions:

Which form of narcissism best fits your mother's behavior?

_____

_____

_____

_____

_____

How does your mother's narcissism effect your mental health?

_____

_____

_____

_____

_____

_____

How have you assimilated the conflicting signals from a hidden narcissist?

_____

_____

_____

_____

_____

_____

How have you attempted to accommodate your mother's wants at your own expense?

_____

_____

_____

_____

_____

_____

_____

How do you react when your mother manipulates you via guilt or withdrawal?

_____

_____

_____

_____

_____

_____

What habits of conduct have you developed as a result of your mother's narcissism?

_____

_____

_____

_____

_____

_____

Life-changing Exercises:

Consider the sort of narcissism your mother exhibits and how it impacts you.

Write about particular situations when you felt manipulated or controlled by your mother.

Identify one manipulative method that your mother does and practice creating limits around it.

Make a list of your personal needs that were overlooked in the partnership.

Practice aggressive communication by expressing your emotions without guilt.

Write a caring letter to yourself, confirming your right to meet your own needs.

Consider how you have absorbed your mother's actions and begin to question those assumptions.

Create a plan for emotionally separating from your mother's manipulative practices.

Set a clear threshold for guilt-based manipulation and regularly enforce it.

Focus on developing connections that generate emotional reciprocity.

CHAPTER 4: WHERE IS DADDY? REST OF THE NARCISSISTIC NEST

Chapter Summary:

This chapter investigates the roles of the father and other family members in a household with a narcissistic mother. Frequently, the father is emotionally or physically unavailable, leaving the daughter to handle her relationship with her mother alone. Fathers may support their daughters by avoiding conflict and neglecting to safeguard them from their mother's narcissism. This chapter also looks at how siblings and extended family members might promote or question the narcissistic dynamics in the home.

Key takeaways:

- Fathers are frequently emotionally or physically absent in narcissistic families.

- Some fathers support the narcissistic mother's actions.

- Daughters may feel abandoned by both of their parents.

- Siblings might fight for acceptance or separate themselves.

- Extended family members may either encourage or dispute the narcissist's dominance.

- The father's role, or lack thereof, has a significant influence on the daughter's sense of security.

- Fathers frequently fail to safeguard girls from their mother's influence.

- Understanding the father's involvement might help girls deal with emotions of abandonment.

Self-Reflective Questions:

How did your father influence the dynamics in your family?

_____

_____

_____

_____

_____

Did you feel emotionally supported by your father, or was he absent?

_____

_____

_____

_____

_____

_____

How did your siblings deal with your mother's narcissism?

_____

_____

_____

_____

_____

_____

_____

What role did extended family members have in sustaining

or challenging the dynamic?

_____

_____

_____

_____

_____

_____

How has your connection with your father influenced your willingness to trust males or authoritative figures?

_____

_____

_____

_____

_____

_____

How have you internalized emotions of abandonment caused by your father's absence?

_____

_____

_____

_____

_____

_____

_____

Life-changing Exercises:

Write about your father's involvement in the family and how it influenced you.

Write a letter to your father and convey any unresolved sentiments.

Consider how your father's absence affected your emotional growth.

Identify any patterns in your interactions with males that resemble those with your father.

Practice forgiveness for your father's flaws, even if it is only for your own recovery.

Examine your connection with your siblings and how it was shaped by family dynamics.

Make a list of how you've sought acceptance from masculine figures in your life.

Set appropriate boundaries with family members that perpetuate poisonous behaviors.

When dealing with feelings of abandonment, remember to be kind to yourself.

Develop trust in relationships via honest communication and vulnerability.

CHAPTER 5: IMAGE IS EVERYTHING: PUT A SMILE ON THAT PRETTY LITTLE FACE

Chapter Summary:

This chapter emphasizes the significance of looks and image in the narcissistic mother's life. Narcissistic moms frequently value appearance above emotion, putting pressure on their daughters to present a flawless image. Daughters are supposed to suppress their feelings and show themselves in a way that reflects well on their mother. This emphasis on image can lead to perfectionism, emotional suppression, and a detachment with the daughter's inner self.

Key takeaways:

- Narcissistic moms value looks over emotional well-being.

- Daughters are frequently expected to keep a beautiful exterior.

- Emotions are suppressed in favor of presenting a positive picture.

- This pressure promotes perfectionism and emotional separation.

- The daughter's identity is linked to how she is regarded by others.

- Daughters may experience difficulty with sincerity and sensitivity as a result.

- The focus on image can lead to anxiety and feelings of inadequacy.

- Healing entails reconnecting with one's authentic self and emotions.

Self-Reflective Questions:

How has your mother's attention to beauty and image influenced your sense of self?

_____

_____

_____

_____

_____

_____

How have you suppressed your emotions to maintain a facade?

_____

_____

_____

_____

_____

_____

How did perfectionism affect your mental health and relationships?

_____

_____

_____

_____

_____

_____

Do you feel pressured to be flawless or project a specific image to the world?

_____

_____

_____

_____

_____

_____

_____

How have you neglected your genuine feelings and needs in favor of keeping appearances?

_____

_____

_____

_____

_____

_____

What would it be like to let go of the need to be flawless and embrace authenticity?

_____

_____

_____

_____

_____

_____

Life-changing Exercises:

Think of times when you felt compelled to maintain a flawless image.

Write about how this pressure has affected your emotional well-being.

Practice expressing your feelings truthfully, even if it is difficult.

Find one area of your life where you can let go of perfectionism.

Create a motto that emphasizes the importance of authenticity above image.

Take a vacation from social media and other venues that perpetuate the need to be flawless.

Write a letter to yourself, recognizing how you've disguised your genuine nature.

Challenge yourself to be vulnerable in a relationship or discussion.

Use mindfulness practices to reconnect with your emotions and authentic self.

Set a goal of embracing imperfection in one area of your life, such as looks, career, or relationships.

CHAPTER 6: TRY SO HARD! THE HIGH-ACHIEVING DAUGHTER

Chapter Summary:

This chapter is about daughters who become great achievers as a response to their mother's narcissism. These girls strive for perfection and achievement in order to earn their mother's favor. While this desire for achievement can lead to professional and personal success, it frequently comes at the expense of the daughter's emotional well-being. The high-achieving daughter is motivated by a fear of failure and a desire for recognition, which can result in exhaustion, anxiety, and an inability to appreciate her achievements.

Key takeaways:

- High-achieving daughters frequently strive for perfection in order to earn their mother's approval.

- This desire for achievement stems from a fear of failure and rejection.

- Daughters may struggle to appreciate their successes because they are constantly seeking approval.

- The quest of perfection can result in burnout and worry.

- High-achieving daughters frequently believe that no amount of accomplishment is ever enough.

- Healing requires reframing success on one's own terms.

- Daughters must learn to find recognition within themselves rather than seeking it from others.

- Letting go of perfectionism is essential for emotional well-being.

Self-Reflective Questions:

What impact has your connection with your mother had on your desire to succeed?

_____

_____

_____

_____

_____

How do you seek affirmation via success or accomplishments?

_____

_____

_____

_____

_____

_____

How has perfectionism impacted your mental health and relationships?

_____

_____

_____

_____

_____

_____

Do you struggle to appreciate your accomplishments, believing that they are never enough?

_____

_____

_____

_____

_____

_____

_____

How would your life change if you stopped aiming for perfection and instead practiced self-compassion?

_____

_____

_____

_____

_____

_____

What would it be like to define success on your own terms, rather than your mother's?

_____

_____

_____

_____

_____

_____

_____

Life-changing Exercises:

Write about your reasons for success and how they connect to your mother's approval.

Make a list of your successes and take time to recognize each one.

Find one area in your life where you can let go of perfectionism.

When you fail to meet your own standards, show yourself compassion.

Set a limit on how hard you work or how committed you are to your accomplishment.

Create a new definition of success that incorporates your ideals and emotional needs.

Consider how your fear of failure has influenced your decisions, then question that fear.

Write a letter to yourself that acknowledges your efforts and provides internal validation.

Take a break from a high-pressure assignment and let yourself relax guilt-free.

Set short, attainable objectives that value your emotional health above perfection.

CHAPTER 7: WHAT'S THE POINT? THE SELF-SABOTAGING DAUGHTER

Chapter Summary:

In this chapter, Dr. McBride investigates daughters who engage in self-destructive activities in response to their narcissistic moms. These girls frequently believe that no matter what they achieve, they will never be good enough, causing them to doubt their own success and happiness. They may postpone, avoid problems, or engage in negative activities that keep them from realizing their full potential. This tendency of self-sabotage is founded in sentiments of unworthiness instilled by years of emotional neglect or criticism from their moms.

Key takeaways:

- Daughters who undermine themselves frequently believe they are unworthy of achievement or happiness.

- They may use delay or avoidance to keep themselves from achieving.

- Self-sabotage is a taught tendency that stems from their mother's criticism or mistreatment.

- These girls may think they are not worthy of love or success.

- Fear of failure or rejection motivates self-destructive behaviors.

- Breaking the cycle of self-sabotage includes facing thoughts of inadequacy.

- Daughters must learn to trust in their own innate worth and potential.

- Healing entails replacing self-sabotage with self-compassion and support.

Self-Reflective Questions:

How has self-sabotage manifested in your life, and where do you believe it originated?

_____

_____

_____

_____

_____

_____

What particular fears or beliefs motivate your self-destructive behaviors?

_____

_____

_____

_____

_____

_____

How did your mother's criticism or neglect affect your sense of self-worth?

_____

_____

_____

_____

_____

_____

What ways do you hold yourself back from realizing your full potential?

_____

_____

_____

_____

_____

_____

How would your life alter if you felt you were deserving of success and happiness?

_____

_____

_____

_____

_____

What is it like to replace self-sabotage with self-compassion?

_____

_____

_____

_____

_____

_____

Life-changing Exercises:

Reflect on moments when you've sabotaged yourself and uncover the underlying anxieties.

Journal about a recent incidence of self-sabotage and investigate how it links to emotions of worthlessness.

Make an action plan to overcome a certain self-destructive behavior.

Try replacing negative self-talk with positive affirmations.

Identify one objective you've been avoiding and make a tiny move toward accomplishing it.

Challenge your fear of failure by actively accepting imperfection in one endeavor.

Develop a regular practice of self-compassion to combat emotions of inadequacy.

Write a letter to your future self, encouraging and believing in your abilities.

Commit to appreciating tiny accomplishments, even if they seem insignificant.

Set a goal to quit procrastinating on one key activity and take action right away.

CHAPTER 8: ROMANTIC FALLOUT: ATTEMPTING TO WIN IN LOVE WHERE I FAILED WITH MOM

Chapter Summary:

This chapter looks at the romantic repercussions of growing up with a narcissistic mother. Daughters frequently pursue relationships in which they unintentionally attempt to "win" the affection they did not receive from their moms. These relationships can be harmful or imbalanced, with daughters either being too forgiving or preferring emotionally unavailable, dominating, or narcissistic spouses. The chapter discusses how unresolved issues with the mother can lead to recurring patterns in romantic relationships and provides strategies for breaking away from these destructive cycles.

Key takeaways:

- Daughters frequently seek affection in romantic relationships that mirror their interactions with their moms.

- They might pick emotionally unavailable or narcissistic spouses.

- These connections demonstrate an unfulfilled desire for mother affection and acceptance.

- Daughters may overgive in relationships to demonstrate their worth.

- Healing entails identifying toxic habits in love relationships.

- Daughters must learn to appreciate themselves regardless of their partner's approval.

- Setting boundaries is critical to stopping the pattern of dysfunctional relationships.

- True healing necessitates acknowledging the unmet desire for mother love.

Self-Reflective Questions:

How have your romantic relationships reflected your bond with your mother?

_____

_____

_____

_____

_____

_____

What tendencies of overgiving or seeking affirmation appear in your relationships?

_____

_____

_____

_____

_____

_____

Have you ever been drawn to emotionally unavailable or narcissistic relationships, and why?

_____

_____

_____

_____

_____

_____

How have unresolved issues with your mother affected your romantic decisions?

_____

_____

_____

_____

_____

_____

How have you neglected your own needs in relationships?

_____

_____

_____

_____

_____

_____

How might your love relationships alter if you truly respected yourself?

_____

_____

_____

_____

_____

_____

Life-changing Exercises:

Reflect on former love relationships and look for patterns that parallel your connection with your mother.

Journal about your unfulfilled need for love and how it manifests itself in your romantic relationships.

Establish a boundary in your present or future relationship that emphasizes your emotional well-being.

To improve your self-esteem outside of relationships, practice self-love and affirmations.

Take a break from dating and focus on repairing the scars caused by your mother.

Identify characteristics of a good relationship and compare them to your previous experiences.

Decide to quit any toxic or one-sided relationships.

Consider what you genuinely need from a love relationship, aside from affirmation.

Create a plan for identifying red flags in potential partners.

Seek therapy or assistance to address the unresolved desire for maternal love that is influencing your relationships.

CHAPTER 9: HELP! I AM BECOMING MY MOTHER: DAUGHTERS AS MOTHERS

Chapter Summary:

This chapter addresses many daughters' worry of becoming like their narcissistic moms once they become parents. Despite their best attempts, many mothers continue to engage in patterns of emotional neglect or control with their own children. This chapter explains how unresolved trauma and unconscious actions can be handed along, but it also gives hope. Dr. McBride emphasizes that self-awareness, conscientious parenting, and healing from the mother's scars may all help to stop the pattern.

Key takeaways:

- Daughters frequently dread becoming like their narcissistic moms when they have children.
- Unresolved trauma can lead to bad practices with one's own children.

- Self-awareness is crucial for ending the cycle of emotional neglect or control.

- Recognizing and resolving emotional triggers is an essential component of conscious parenting.

- Daughters can overcome their history and become compassionate, supporting moms.

- Healing the mother wound is critical for disrupting generational patterns.

- Daughters must learn to parent in ways that respect their children's emotional needs.

- Self-compassion and treatment can help you avoid repeating detrimental habits.

Self-Reflective Questions:

In what ways do you dread being like your mother as a parent?

_____

_____

_____

_____

_____

How do unresolved issues with your mother influence your parenting style?

_____

_____

_____

_____

_____

_____

What emotional triggers occur when you are parenting, and where do they originate?

_____

_____

_____

_____

_____

_____

How do you actively end the pattern of emotional neglect or control in your family?

_____

_____

_____

_____

_____

_____

What actions can you take to support your child's emotional well-being?

_____

_____

_____

_____

_____

How would your connection with your children alter if you were completely healed from your past?

_____

_____

_____

_____

_____

_____

Life-changing Exercises:

Think of times when you felt or acted like your mother with your children.

Journal about your anxieties of duplicating your mother's habits and how you can deal with them.

Determine which parenting behavior you wish to improve and devise a plan to achieve it.

Conscious parenting is being emotionally present with your children.

Seek therapy or support groups to help you work through underlying trauma.

Reflect on your children's emotional needs and how you may better address them.

Write a letter to your children, stating your desire to be a supporting and caring parent.

When you make errors as a parent, practice self-compassion and remember that mending takes time.

Make a list of ways you may nourish yourself emotionally in order to avoid parental burnout.

Create a daily mindfulness practice to help you stay present and emotionally connected with your children.

CHAPTER 10: INITIAL STEPS: HOW IT FEELS, NOT HOW IT LOOKS

Chapter Summary:

This chapter focuses on the first steps in recovery from a narcissistic mother's influence. Dr. McBride emphasizes that healing is not about external appearances, but about how you feel within. Many daughters of narcissistic moms have learnt to value appearance, but genuine healing requires reconnecting with your emotions and allowing yourself to feel fully. This chapter explains how to start your journey by admitting your suffering, allowing yourself to mourn, and accepting that it's alright to feel.

Key takeaways:

- Healing from narcissistic mothering begins with a focus on how you feel, not how things appear.
- Many daughters are taught to repress their feelings and emphasize looks.

- Accepting and allowing yourself to feel your suffering is the first step toward recovery.

- Grieving the death of the mother you never had is necessary.

- Allow yourself to feel profoundly, even if it is uncomfortable.

- Healing requires time and self-compassion.

- You must reinvent your identity based on internal feelings rather than outward affirmation.

- True emotional freedom stems from connecting with and expressing your emotions.

Self-Reflective Questions:

How have you valued looks above your genuine emotions?

_____

_____

_____

_____

_____

What emotions have you suppressed, and why?

_____

_____

_____

_____

_____

What would your life be like if you were free to feel profoundly and express your emotions?

_____

_____

_____

_____

_____

What losses have you suffered as a result of your connection with your mother, and have you mourned them?

_____

_____

_____

_____

_____

How do you believe concentrating on your inner world, rather than external affirmation, will affect your recovery process?

_____

_____

_____

_____

_____

_____

What worries occur when you consider shedding the mask and accepting your actual feelings?

_____

_____

_____

_____

_____

_____

Life-changing Exercises:

Write about how you've emphasized appearances and how this has affected your emotional well-being.

Identify one feeling that you have been repressing and allow yourself to completely experience and express it.

Write a letter to yourself, allowing yourself to mourn the loss of the mother you never had.

Mindfulness or meditation might help you reconnect with your emotions.

Commit to sharing one honest feeling with someone you trust, even if it seems vulnerable.

Make a list of things you've done for appearances' sake and think about how you can emphasize honesty.

Take time each day to check in with your emotions and allow yourself to experience whatever arises.

Consider how your healing process might differ if you focused exclusively on how you felt rather than how things appeared.

Make a safe area where you may express your feelings without being judged.

Create a mantra that foster emotional honesty and internal affirmation.

CHAPTER 11: PART OF AND APART FROM: SEPARATION FROM MOTHER

Chapter Summary:

This chapter dives into the emotional separation from a narcissistic mother. Daughters frequently feel intertwined with their moms, unsure where their mother stops and they begin. Dr. McBride emphasizes the necessity of maintaining emotional space and setting appropriate boundaries. Separation is not about eliminating links, but about discovering your own identity and acknowledging that your mother's actions does not represent your value. The chapter provides ways for establishing boundaries and overcoming the shame that typically comes with emotional isolation.

Key takeaways:

- Emotional detachment from a narcissistic mother is necessary for recovery.

- Daughters frequently identify with their moms and struggle to create their own identities.

- Healthy boundaries are essential for maintaining your emotional well-being.

- Emotional separation does not always imply breaking off touch, but rather establishing distance and autonomy.

- Recognizing that your mother's actions does not represent your worth is critical.

- Guilt is common after emotional separation, but it's critical to prioritize your healing.

- Developing your own identity apart from your mother's influence is an important stage in the process.

- Separation is about restoring one's individuality and emotional independence.

Self-Reflective Questions:

How have you battled to establish your own identity apart from your mother?

_____

_____

_____

_____

_____

In what ways do you feel connected to your mother's needs, feelings, and expectations?

_____

_____

_____

_____

_____

_____

What limits can you create to safeguard your emotional health?

_____

_____

_____

_____

_____

How does shame manifest when you consider building emotional distance from your mother?

_____

_____

_____

_____

_____

How would your life alter if you completely dissociated
emotionally and established your own identity?

_____

_____

_____

_____

_____

What anxieties or problems arise when you consider setting
limits with your mother?

_____

_____

_____

_____

_____

Life-changing Exercises:

Consider how your relationship with your mother has shaped your sense of self.

Journal about strategies to emotionally disconnect from your mother while yet retaining a relationship, if desired.

Create a list of boundaries to preserve your emotional well-being.

Practice saying "no" to your mother's wants and expectations in little ways.

Consider how your mother's actions is not representative of your worth or value.

Seek aid from a therapist or a support group to go through the emotional separation process.

Write a letter to yourself expressing your right to autonomy and emotional independence.

Determine one area of your life where you may begin recovering your identity.

Set a goal to prioritize your own wants and feelings over your mother's demands.

Develop ways for dealing with the shame that may result from setting limits and generating distance.

CHAPTER 12: BECOMING THE WOMAN I TRULY AM: DESERVED DAUGHTERS

Chapter Summary:

In this chapter, Dr. McBride highlights the significance of accepting your value and appreciating the woman you actually are. Daughters of narcissistic moms frequently have feelings of inadequacy and a strong perception that they are unworthy of love, success, or pleasure. This chapter encourages daughters to question their beliefs and rediscover their sense of self-worth. It emphasizes self-acceptance, self-love, and learning to trust your own voice. Healing is accepting the fact that you are worthy of love and respect simply because you exist.

Key takeaways:

- Daughters of narcissistic moms typically experience emotions of inadequacy and unworthiness.

- Reclaiming your self-worth is an important part of rehabilitation.

- Regardless matter how your mother treats you, you deserve to be loved, successful, and happy.

- Self-acceptance is vital for accepting the authentic woman you are.

- Healing is fighting the notion that you are unworthy of wonderful things in life.

- Learning to trust your own voice and instincts is critical.

- Self-love and self-compassion are essential for emotional rehabilitation.

- You are valuable just because you exist, not because of your accomplishments or how you are viewed.

Self-Reflective Questions:

How have you dealt with thoughts of inadequacy or unworthiness, and where do they stem from?

_____

_____

_____

_____

_____

How have you felt undeserving of love, success, or happiness?

_____

_____

_____

_____

_____

How would your life alter if you totally believed that you deserve everything good?

_____

_____

_____

_____

_____

What ideas about yourself do you need to question in order to recover your self-worth?

_____

_____

_____

_____

_____

_____

How can you increase your faith in your own voice and intuition?

_____

_____

_____

_____

_____

What measures can you take to develop self-love and compassion?

_____

_____

_____

_____

_____

Life-changing Exercises:

Reflect on how you've absorbed sentiments of unworthiness and confront those ideas.

Make a list of affirmations that emphasize your value and deserving of love and happiness.

Write a letter to yourself that expresses self-love and acceptance.

Practice following your intuition in little decisions and consider how it feels.

Create a daily self-compassion practice, like meditation or writing.

Identify one area of your life in which you may begin to accept your value and worthy.

Write down all of the reasons you feel you are worthy, without any qualifications.

Seek out therapy or support groups to assist you overcome feelings of inadequacy.

Self-care might help you feel more worthy of love and attention.

Set a goal to prioritize your emotional and mental health, understanding that you deserve to be cared for and healed.

CHAPTER 13: MY TURN: DEALING WITH MOTHER IN RECOVERY

Chapter Summary:

This chapter discusses how to handle your connection with your narcissistic mother while you are recuperating. As daughters attempt to recover from the emotional harm caused by their moms, they frequently find it difficult to negotiate interactions with the mother, especially if the mother stays narcissistic and unchanging. Dr. McBride offers advice on how to create limits, manage expectations, and safeguard your development while dealing with a tough mother.

Key takeaways:

- Dealing with a narcissistic mother throughout recovery might be difficult but necessary.

- Setting and keeping clear boundaries is critical to safeguarding your recovery process.

- Your mother may not change, but you can control how you deal with her.

- Managing your expectations for your mother's conduct helps you prevent disappointment.

- You must put your emotional well-being before pleasing or appeasing your mother.

- Healing is knowing how to protect yourself emotionally during conversations with your mother.

- Boundaries allow you to retain the progress you've made in your recovery.

- It's critical to recognize that you may never get the affection or acceptance you want from your mother.

Self-Reflective Questions:

How did you handle your connection with your mother while working on your recovery?

_____

_____

_____

_____

_____

_____

What limits should you establish to safeguard your emotional well-being?

_____

_____

_____

_____

_____

_____

How have your expectations of your mother changed as you sought to heal?

_____

_____

_____

_____

_____

In what ways do you continue to seek validation or acceptance from your mother?

_____

_____

_____

_____

_____

_____

How can you put your own health over pleasing your mother?

_____

_____

_____

_____

_____

_____

What would it be like to realize that your mother may never change?

_____

_____

_____

_____

_____

_____

Life-changing Exercises:

Consider how you handled encounters with your mother during your recovery journey.

Journal about the limits you need to establish with your mother to protect your advancement.

Make a plan for dealing with challenging encounters with your mother while maintaining your emotional equilibrium.

Say "no" to your mother's requests or manipulations in tiny ways.

Write down your expectations for your mother and how they have changed as you have recovered.

Set a goal to avoid seeking validation or approval from your mother and instead focus on self-acceptance.

Make a list of tactics for emotionally protecting yourself when interacting with your mother.

Consider how your recovery has influenced how you perceive your connection with your mother.

Practice becoming detached from your mother's ideas or critiques.

Create a mantra that emphasizes your autonomy and emotional independence from your mother's influence.

CHAPTER 14: FILLING THE EMPTY MIRROR: ENDING THE NARCISSISTIC LEGACY

Chapter Summary:

Dr. McBride's last chapter focuses on how daughters might break the cycle of narcissistic mothering and mend the "empty mirror" within them. The "empty mirror" represents the girls' lack of emotional reflection and validation while growing up. This chapter urges girls to take full responsibility for their own rehabilitation and to establish a new legacy for themselves and their children. Daughters may break the cycle of narcissism and build a better future for their family by meeting their own emotional needs and being the people they've always wanted to be.

Key takeaways:

- The "empty mirror" symbolizes the emotional emptiness created by a narcissistic mother.

- Healing requires girls to accept responsibility for meeting their own emotional needs.

- Ending the narcissistic legacy means halting the cycle for future generations.

- Daughters must learn to affirm and reflect their own value, rather than seeking external approval.

- Self-awareness and compassion are essential for establishing a new emotional legacy.

- Daughters can modify their family's emotional patterns by intentional action.

- True healing is forming a new identity that matches the woman they've always wished to be.

- Healing is a continual process that leads to a more fulfilled and emotionally healthy existence.

Self-Reflective Questions:

How have you encountered the "empty mirror" in your life, and how has it impacted you?

_____

_____

_____

_____

_____

What emotional needs have you been attempting to meet outside, and how might you address them internally?

_____

_____

_____

_____

_____

_____

In what ways do you intend to disrupt the narcissistic cycle for yourself and your family?

_____

_____

_____

_____

_____

How would your life alter if you accepted complete responsibility for your emotional well-being?

_____

_____

_____

_____

_____

How can you affirm yourself and develop a healthy emotional identity?

_____

_____

_____

_____

_____

_____

How can you avoid passing on narcissistic mothering practices to the next generation?

_____

_____

_____

_____

_____

_____

Life-changing Exercises:

Consider how the "empty mirror" has influenced your sense of self and emotional needs.

Journal about how you may accept responsibility for filling your own emotional holes.

Create a list of strategies to validate yourself without relying on external approval.

Identify the precise narcissistic patterns you wish to avoid handing on to future generations.

Write a letter to your future self, stating your desire to eliminate the narcissistic legacy.

Recognize your own healing process to practice self-compassion.

Create a self-care practice that prioritizes your emotional and mental needs.

Create a vision for the woman you want to be and take one step toward achieving it each day.

Consider how you may model good emotional conduct for your children or loved ones.

Set a goal to check in with yourself emotionally on a regular basis and avoid seeking external approval.

SELF-EVALUATION QUESTIONS

How has my connection with my mother affected my self-esteem and sense of self?

_____

_____

_____

_____

_____

How have I valued exterior looks above my interior emotional well-being?

_____

_____

_____

_____

_____

_____

What patterns from my connection with my mother have I unintentionally duplicated in my other relationships?

_____

_____

_____

_____

_____

How frequently do I seek affirmation from others, and how does this impact my confidence and happiness?

_____

_____

_____

_____

_____

Have I set good boundaries with my mother, and how do I deal with feelings of guilt when I do?

_____

_____

_____

_____

_____

_____

Do I find myself overachieving for acceptance or destroying my own achievement out of emotions of inadequacy?

_____

_____

_____

_____

_____

_____

How has my connection with my mother influenced my romantic relationships and expectations of love?

_____

_____

_____

_____

_____

In what ways do I dread becoming like my mother, and how can I stop the cycle?

_____

_____

_____

_____

_____

Have I allowed myself to mourn the loss of the caring mother I never had, and how has this affected my healing?

_____

_____

_____

_____

_____

How do I deal with my emotions? Do I repress, ignore, or overcompensate for them?

_____

_____

_____

_____

_____

_____

What efforts have I done to emotionally disconnect from my mother and establish my own identity?

_____

_____

_____

_____

_____

_____

How do I perceive myself? Do I believe I am deserving of love, happiness, and success, or do I feel inadequate?

_____

_____

_____

_____

_____

_____

Am I willing to let go of the desire for my mother's approval in order to truly heal and progress?

_____

_____

_____

_____

_____

_____

What particular activities can I take to prevent the emotional patterns of narcissistic mothering from being passed down to future generations?

_____

_____

_____

_____

_____

_____

How can I prioritize my recovery path while still accepting full responsibility for addressing the emotional gap left by my mother?

_____

_____

_____

_____

_____

_____

_____

_____

_____

_____

_____

_____

_____

_____

Made in the USA
Middletown, DE
16 December 2024